# Take a trip to
# RUSSIA

Keith Lye

*General Editor*

Henry Pluckrose

Franklin Watts

London   New York   Sydney   Toronto

# Words about Russia

Baikal, Lake
Baku
Black Sea
Bolsheviks
Bolshoi Theatre
Bukhara

Caspian Sea
Caucasus
  Mountains
classical ballet
Communist
collectives

Dnieper
Don

Kara Kum
Kiev
kopek
Kremlin

Leningrad

mausoleum
Moscow
Moslems
mosques

Odessa

rouble

Samarkand
Siberia
Sochi
Socialist
  Republic
Soviet Union

Tashkent

Ukraine
USSR

Vladivostok
*Vostok 1*

Young Pioneer

Franklin Watts Limited
12a Golden Square
London W1

ISBN UK edition: 0 85166 964 6
ISBN US edition: 0 531 04472–6
Library of Congress Catalog Card No:
82–50062

© Franklin Watts Limited 1982

Reprinted 1983

Typeset by Ace Filmsetting Ltd.,
Frome, Somerset
Printed in Great Britain by
E. T. Heron, Essex and London

Maps: Tony Payne
Design and Editorial Services:
Grub Street
Photographs: Zefa; D. Turner, 8.

Russia is the world's largest country. One-fourth of Russia is in Europe. The rest is in Asia. The Trans-Siberian Railway is 9,300 km (5,800 miles) long. It links the capital city, Moscow, in European Russia, with the port of Vladivostok, in Eastern Asia.

The Kremlin, the old citadel (fortress) of Moscow, stands on the north bank of the Moskva River. It contains old palaces and churches and it houses Russia's government.

Red Square, next to the Kremlin wall in Moscow, contains the tomb of Vladimir Lenin. Lenin led the Bolsheviks in the Russian Revolution of November 1917, when Russia became a Communist country.

Saint Basil's Church in Moscow's Red Square has a total of eight, onion-shaped domes. This Church was built between 1555 and 1561.

GUM in central Moscow is one of the world's largest stores. Like all stores in Russia, it is owned by the government which pays the wages of the people who work in them. The government also owns all factories and most of the land.

This picture shows some Russian stamps and money. There are 100 kopeks in each rouble. The government does not allow Russian money to be taken out of the country.

Lake Baikal, in central Siberia, freezes over for four months every year. It is more than 1600 metres (1 mile) deep and the world's deepest lake. Siberia covers much of Asian Russia. Central Siberia contains huge forests, the home of bears and wolves.

The Kara Kum Desert lies east of the Caspian Sea in southern Russia. Kara Kum means "black sands" even though the sand here is golden-brown. Russia also has many mountain ranges, such as the Caucasus which run between the Black Sea and the Caspian Sea.

Russia has vast wheat fields. It grows more wheat than any other country. Farm workers on government farms are paid wages. But on other large farms, called collectives, the people do not get wages. Instead they share the produce between them.

Here people are shopping at a market in Rostov. This city lies on the Don, a river that flows into the Sea of Azov. This sea is linked to the Black Sea and the Mediterranean Sea.

This village with its wooden church is in an area of rich farmland called the Ukraine. It is in the south-west and is one of the 15 republics of the Union of Soviet Socialist Republics, Russia's official name. It is also called the USSR or the Soviet Union.

Odessa, a seaport on the Black Sea, is also in the Ukraine. It exports grain, sugar, wood and wool. It has many large factories.

This lumber yard on the outskirts of Moscow is supplied with wood from the forests which surround the city. Forests cover about one-third of Russia. The government owns most of the forests.

This factory makes steel. Russia produces more steel than any other country. It has many resources. It leads the world in producing coal, oil, iron ore and several other metals. These raw materials are used in Russian factories. Today 47 out of every 100 people work in industry.

17

These children live in Tashkent, a city in the Asian part of Russia. A child who wears a red scarf belongs to a youth organization called the Young Pioneers. Teachers take away the scarf of any child who misbehaves.

In cities most families live in small apartments. After a day's work, many Russians enjoy watching television. Sport, especially soccer and ice hockey, is extremely popular.

This is a street scene in Samarkand, one of the oldest cities in central Asia, where its customs have mainly remained unchanged. The area produces mainly wheat, silk and cotton, but also tungsten.

Ballets are performed at the Bolshoi Theatre in Moscow. Russia is the home of classical ballet. There are 36 major ballet companies. Many people think that performances at the Bolshoi of such classical ballets as *Swan Lake* are the best in the world.

People enjoy green tea and food at an open-air meeting place in Bukhara, in the Asian part of Russia. It has a warm, dry climate. There are large, hot deserts between Bukhara and the Caspian Sea.

Tomatoes, grapes and cucumbers are sold at a market in Bukhara. Many people in Bukhara are Moslems. South of Bukhara are the Moslem countries of Afghanistan and Iran.

Moslem mosques can be seen in the city of Bukhara. Russia contains many different people and races who have varied customs. More than 60 major languages are spoken.

Many villages contain old houses of wood. They have steep roofs so that snow will not pile up on them. They often have decorated windows.

Leningrad is the second largest Russian city. This picture shows its University. It is an important port on the Gulf of Finland. Once called St. Petersburg, it was renamed Leningrad or "Lenin's city" in 1917 after the Russian Revolution.

Kiev is Russia's third largest city. It stands on the Dnieper River in the Ukraine. It is called "the mother of Russian cities". It was Russia's chief city from the 900s to the 1200s.

Baku, a city with just over one million people, is in the middle of an oil-producing area. It stands on the western shore of the Caspian Sea. The Caspian Sea contains salty water, but is completely surrounded by land and so it is really a lake. In fact it is the largest lake in the world.

Sochi is one of Russia's leading seaside resorts. It is on the eastern coast of the Black Sea. It has many comfortable modern hotels.

Parades are held in the huge Red Square in Moscow on May 1 (May Day) and on November 7. Rockets and other weapons are on show.

The Russian TU-144 Supersonic Airliner was built to fly faster than the speed of sound. Russia has many fine scientists, designers and engineers. Russia was the first country to put a man in space in 1961. He was Yuri Gagarin. His spacecraft was called *Vostok 1*.

# Index

Asian Russia 3, 10, 18, 22
Azov, Sea of 13

Baku 28
Ballet 20
Black Sea 13, 15, 29
Bolshoi Ballet 20
Bukhara 22–24

Caspian Sea 11, 22, 28
Caucasus Mountains 11

Dnieper River 27
Don River 13

Farming 12
Forests 10, 16

Gagarin, Yuri 31
GUM 7

Homes 19
Houses 25

Industry 17

Kara Kum Desert 11
Kiev 27
Kremlin 4, 5

Lake Baikal 10
Languages 24

Lenin, Vladimir 5
Leningrad 26

Money 8
Moscow 3–7, 20
Moslems 23–24

Odessa 15

Red Square 5–6, 30
Russian Revolution 5, 26
Rostov 13

St Basil's Church 6
Samarkand 21
School 18
Siberia 10
Sochi 29
Stamps 8

Tashkent 18
Trans-Siberian
   Railway 3, 10
TU-144 Supersonic
   Airliner 31

Ukraine 14–15, 27

Vladivostok 3
*Vostok 1* 31

Young Pioneers 18